Be Smart

Don't Start

A Vaping Prevention Tool for Children
By Katelyn Brooke Shepherd

Be Smart
Don't Start

A Vaping Prevention Tool for Children
By Katelyn Brooke Shepherd

Meet Katelyn Brooke Shepherd, a nurse from the southern part of West Virginia who loves reading and spreading knowledge to others. During her time as a school nurse, she has seen the scary spread of vaping, even among little kids. As a parent and a nurse, she knows that education is key to help kids dodge the dangers of e-cigarettes. That's why she's on a mission to spread awareness and teach young minds about the risks of vaping. Katelyn's goal is to empower kids to say NO to vaping and staying healthy so they can be the best selves they possibly can.

Hello my name is Stacy and I am in 5th grade
Today I have a story about a big decision that I made

I ride the bus in the evening
it was a day like any other
Until TJ came up to me on the bus
And told me he had something he stole from his brother

He said it tasted like candy
so yummy and so sweet
He told me to try a   "hit "from the vape
That I would like it and it can't be beat

Thank goodness the bus had stopped
And sent me on my way
Because honestly it kind of scared me
And I didn't know what to say

My mom saw I was upset.

But she couldn't figure out why

So she asked me what was wrong

And I started to cry

I told my mom about everything

How TJ offered me a vape

And my mom assured me I did the right thing

Because they are not safe

My mom started to explain
How vapes can make kids sick
How companies target their products to kids
And how it makes no sense

Vapes have a drug called nicotine in them
And once you start it's hard to stop
They can make you go down a bad path
One filled with danger and the cops

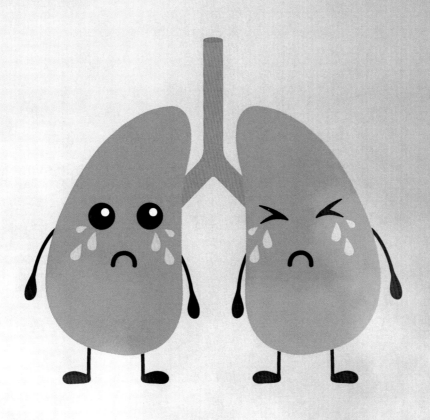

They are also filled with chemicals

Ones that our lungs do not enjoy

They cause a lot of damage in the body

And do not care what they destroy

Mom explained that once this happens
The damage is permeant, and cannot be undone
That it might look cool and fun to do
But addiction can happen to anyone

Addiction is like a monster

That controls and takes over your mind

It makes you do and say a lot of things

That are mean and unkind

It may start off with vaping
But end in something more
Because nicotine is a gateway drug
For others to start to explore

And although adults may do these things
It still is not safe
Especially for young and growing minds
It's never okay to vape

If you ever see someone you know

Decide to smoke a vape at school

You should automatically go tell a teacher

And tell them "hey that's not cool"

You do not have to give a special reason

If someone asks you to vape

Just tell them   "no thank you I do not want to"

And cut to the chase

Mom called the school the next morning
To let them know what TJ had done
And after his mom gave him the same talk
He knew he had done very wrong

He apologized to me the next morning

Telling me he never knew

That vaping was a serious and dangerous thing

For everyone including me and you

Now I feel all better
And know how to stay safe
By saying no to these things
And staying away from vapes!

The End

Made in United States
North Haven, CT
13 March 2024

49939681R00024